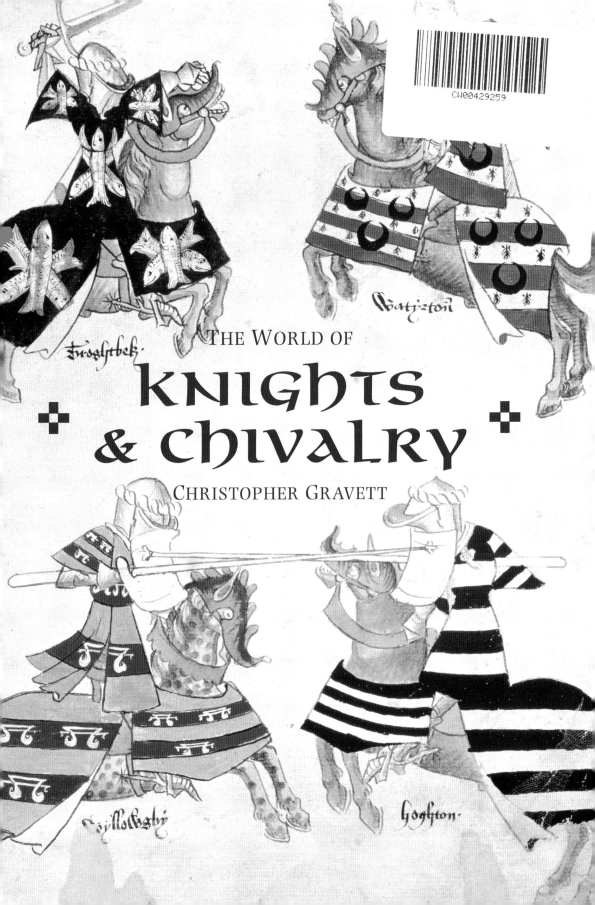

The World of

KNIGHTS
& CHIVALRY

CHRISTOPHER GRAVETT

IMPORTANT DATES

1066 The Normans invade Anglo-Saxon England; William the Conqueror begins castle-building

1085 William orders the Domesday Book, as a survey of his kingdom

1135–54 Civil wars between Stephen and Matilda

1190 Many English knights join the Third Crusade under Richard I

1215 King John grants the Magna Carta to the barons

1216 Civil wars between King John and his barons; death of King John

1265 Simon de Montfort calls the first parliament but is killed in the same year at the Battle of Evesham

1277 Edward I of England invades Wales for the first time; castle-building in Wales begins

1297 The English force is defeated by the Scots under William Wallace at Stirling Bridge

1298 Edward I defeats Wallace at Falkirk

1314 The Scots under Robert the Bruce defeat the English at Bannockburn

1330 The Scots are defeated at Dupplin Moor

1337 The Hundred Years War between England and France begins

1340 The English Navy win a sea battle against the French off Sluys

1346 Edward III defeats the French forces at Crécy

1348–50 The Black Death kills up to one-third of England's population

1356 The Black Prince captures King John of France in the battle at Poitiers

1388 The Peasants' Revolt is led by Wat Tyler

1415 Henry V defeats the French at Agincourt

1429 French cavalry catch and defeat a small English army at Patay, before they can form into position

1430 Joan of Arc defeats the English besiegers of Orleans in France

1453 The Hundred Years War ends and English forces are evicted from France

1455 The Wars of the Roses begin between the royal houses of York and Lancaster

1461 At Towton, the Lancastrians lose the bloodiest battle ever fought in England

1485 At the Battle of Bosworth, the Yorkist King Richard III is killed by Henry Tudor, effectively ending the Wars of the Roses

1531 Henry VIII takes the title 'Supreme head of the English Church', and breaks with Rome

1536 Henry VIII begins the dissolution of the monasteries

1588 The Spanish Armada is defeated in its bid to invade England

1642 The English Civil Wars begin between Charles I and Parliament

1649 Charles I is tried and executed

1651 The Civil Wars come to an end

1660 Charles II is restored to the English throne

ᴍᴇᴅɪᴇᴠᴀʟ knights are generally imagined to be chivalrous horsemen in shining armour, honouring ladies, serving the Church and protecting the weak. Knighthood included men from all walks of life, from the king to the landless adventurer. Early knights were often illiterate and sometimes brutish, but over the centuries many became cultured, affected by chivalric ideals and influenced by the Church, by the arts and by learning legal skills. When warfare changed, their rank ensured they maintained their position as commanders and men of standing in society, the title of 'knight', even today, being a reward for service to the country.

Knights had first appeared in France in the 8th and 9th centuries, in response to the collapse of royal power and attacks from Viking raiders. Many freemen joined noblemen for protection, where they were expected to become mounted warriors and fight, in return for land or a place in the household. In some parts of Europe, knighthood appeared later, or in different forms. Knights made their mark in England in 1066, as elite mounted troops in the invading army of Duke William of Normandy. The conquered English noticed such warriors following their leaders, and used the Anglo-Saxon word for a serving man – 'cniht'.

TOP AND ABOVE Mounted Norman knights in the invading army of Duke William of Normandy ride into battle at Hastings in 1066, from the Bayeux Tapestry.

3

✦ DEFENDING THE CASTLE ✦

STONE castles were built in Britain by the Norman invaders in 1066. Lords had begun fortifying their homes during the unrest in France in the 9th and 10th centuries and the castle remained both a private residence and a stronghold. Following the Norman Conquest, castles provided a secure base for assembling troops and from which knights could control an area of about 20 miles (32km) radius, the distance an armed man could comfortably ride out and back in a day. They were placed in towns and cities to remind the English who was in charge, and some became the headquarters of the county sheriff, the king's representative. Castles also blocked access along borders, for if an invader wanted control he had to take every stronghold in the area, wasting time and men in sieges. Meanwhile, knights could ride out to harass his forces and prevent the seizure of food for the enemy troops.

Knights spent part of their feudal service guarding their lord's strongholds, although this could sometimes be changed to money to

ABOVE The great motte raised at Cardiff Castle by Robert Fitzhamon in the 12th century within the old Roman fort.

LEFT The great hall and gallery of Hedingham Castle keep, in Essex, probably built for entertaining by Aubrey de Vere, to celebrate becoming Earl of Essex in 1142.

pay professional soldiers. Thus all castles were symbols of power but they were more than that. They were meeting places to hold court, to hear disputes and to dispense justice. Kings and aristocrats owned a number of castles and might use them as secure rest areas during a journey. Many castles spent their entire history at peace.

The earliest castles usually consisted of an enclosure or bailey protected by a ditch, earthen rampart and timber palisade. Inside was a hall where everyone lived, with a private area for the family, kitchens, workshops, barns and stores. Many such castles also had a great mound of rammed earth, the 'motte', topped with a palisade and tower. Rectangular stone keeps ('donjons' or great towers) also appeared. Gradually, stone

walls replaced much of the timber and, in the 12th century, the number of stone keeps increased; some were simply for ceremonial use. By the later 12th century, new castles were being built without a keep, relying on strong flanking towers jutting out, to allow archers to shoot along the main walls. Existing castles might be upgraded or extended.

By the 13th century cylindrical towers were becoming popular, whose curved surfaces left no sharp corners for an enemy miner's pickaxe and eliminated blind spots at the corners of the battlements. Huge gatehouses developed, with enormous towers protecting a passage that was fitted with all manner of defensive tricks such as drawbridges or turning bridges, iron-shod portcullises, double doors and so-called 'murder holes' in the passage roof. Some of the most powerful castles were built in Wales by Edward I in the second half of the 13th century. From the 14th century, gun ports were introduced to mount small cannon.

However, only a few castles were besieged during the Wars of the Roses in the later 15th century.

Castles had always been residences – even Edward I's great fortress at Conwy, in Wales, had a garden – and as social conditions changed they were increasingly adapted for comfort with larger windows, while the keep evolved into a private residential tower. The new 16th-century 'castles' built by Henry VIII were garrison forts packed with cannon, no longer private residences. Many castles were slighted after the English Civil Wars (1642–51) but those that did not fall into decay were adapted as stately residences.

Feudal service

Feudalism was based on service, in return for land or shelter. In England, the king granted large estates known as an 'honor' to his principal lords (his tenants-in-chief). In return, they provided fighting men to the king and, similarly, knights served them during war and in peacetime. Land was worked by peasants.

KEEPING THE PEACE

KNIGHTS had a key role in English life, especially the king and his most powerful noblemen, who were also knights. From the 12th century, able knights were recruited into government, becoming learned in law and administration, gaining wealth and often marrying into powerful families. They sat in the shire courts and became known as knights of the shire. In 1265 Simon de Montfort bolstered his revolt against Henry III by summoning knights and townsmen (burgesses) to his great council, in this way sowing the seeds of parliament, a practice which continued after the revolt was crushed. However, parliament added to the pressures already on the knights and as these increased, many refused to be knighted;

by the 15th century, only about 5–10 per cent of the king's army were knights.

The king's council meetings were echoed in the feudal courts to which noblemen summoned their knights. As lords of the manor on their own estates, knights held court to deal out justice and received free labour by peasants on their farms. However, peasant status could change for better or worse.

A knight could employ large numbers of people if he was wealthy: castellans to run his castles (great noblemen owned several) and marshals to organize fighting men and horses; chamberlains and clerks to deal with documents; stewards, butlers, cooks, brewers, huntsmen, falconers,

ABOVE Hunting deer, from Gaston Phoebus' *Livre de Chasse*.

RIGHT Lord Luttrell's falconer, from the *Luttrell Psalter*.

Hunting & dining

Knights enjoyed hunting and hawking. Hunting also added a variety of foods at mealtimes. Beef, mutton, pork, fowl, fish and game were eaten, vegetables usually being peas or beans. A light breakfast was followed by the main meal in the middle of the day, with supper in the evening. The rich used gold and silver plate but others placed food on a flat slab of stale bread, which might be given to the poor afterwards. Meals were enlivened by music, minstrels and strolling entertainers.

ABOVE John of Gaunt feasted by the King of Portugal. Food is brought via a serving hatch while musicians entertain.

BELOW Knights playing chess, detail from a 15th-century manuscript.

dog-keepers and even warreners, for the warrens where rabbits were kept for eating. A knight's wife might be a lady-in-waiting to a great lady, and could also run her husband's estate in his absence. The king sometimes granted areas of forest to his lords (and poaching carried harsh punishments).

Knights were often keen to acquire a town house; walled towns offered protection from enemies, shire courts came to be held there and the county sheriff represented the king. Towns also allowed access to markets and to rarer commodities: fine silks and spices from the East, and herbs. The wealthiest lords created new towns, such as Cardiff, Wells and Chesterfield in feudal England, gave them charters and enjoyed part of their profits. They might also give gifts of money to religious buildings, such as abbeys, churches and chapels, sometimes to atone for violent crimes.

ALL knights needed to be taught how to wear armour, wield weapons and to ride. Training is at first little documented, and even in the 12th century relatively little is known. A boy – sometimes as young as seven – was often taken away from his home and placed with a lord (perhaps a relative) or even the king. As a page, he learned the basic routine of cleaning equipment, working with horses, handling armour and weapons, even perhaps some rudimentary reading and writing from the castle chaplain. He might also learn some manners, for instance, how to behave in the company of ladies.

At around the age of 14, he became a squire (also known as a valet). He learned to fight, perhaps with

ABOVE A 15th-century depiction of the creation of a knight, dubbed on the shoulders with the flat edge of a sword and fitted with gold spurs, his banner held aloft.

LEFT A knight trains at the quintain; the hanging bar will swing round when the shield is struck and test his skill in avoiding it.

8

A knight's spurs

Knights were needed to lead troops, so they were sometimes created before a battle, which also encouraged them to fight better. Edward, the Black Prince won his knightly spurs after the battle of Crécy. However, many were content to remain squires and were never knighted; nevertheless they would fight in a battle or compete in a tournament. Other knights were disinclined to war and paid scutage (shield money) to their lord, to hire professional soldiers instead.

overweight weapons to build his muscles, practising at wooden posts, dummies or against other squires or knights. Sometimes a squire sat astride a wooden horse pulled along by other squires, to test his skill with a lance. Squires also wrestled, threw spears, hurled rocks and went hunting. They learnt singing, dancing and other peaceful accomplishments, and how to carve meat at table. They were taught to ride the lively stallions used as warhorses, controlling them with their knees and spurs to free their hands for battle. When on the march, they put up the tents and went foraging.

The 13th-century Templar Rule shows that many of the squires were only servants. It describes how, on the march, two squires would go in front laden with equipment and leading the horses. Before battle, one youth handed the knight his shield and lance, while the other waited behind with a spare warhorse. As they grew older, squires accompanied the knight to battle or the tournament, pulling him out of the press if wounded, and helping him to remount if he had fallen off his horse.

At around the age of 21, squires who were noblemen would be knighted. Until the 12th century this ceremony was performed by another knight. Later, in the 16th century, Queen Elizabeth I made it the exclusive right of the monarch. The squire received the 'dub', which was a symbolic cuff, perhaps to remember the knight performing the ceremony. Later, the cuff was replaced with a tap from the flat of a sword. As time passed, the ceremony became more elaborate, and increasingly involved the Church. The young squire might stand vigil all night with his sword on the altar, receive a mattress, and be given a ritual bath to cleanse him before being dressed in new robes in symbolic colours. His sword was blessed and belted round him (sometimes by the sovereign himself). New knights often went out to demonstrate their prowess, perhaps in a tournament.

A feudal lord could ask for a contribution from his men when his eldest son was knighted. From the 13th century, the increasing expense of equipment and the ceremony, the affluent lifestyle often expected, together with extra burdens on knights such as government work, attending courts and parliament, resulted in a reluctance to be knighted. The king found it necessary to pass Laws of Attainder, to force eligible men into knighthood.

ABOVE Training at the pel, a wooden post for practising weapon skills, from a 13th-century version of a Roman military treatise.

A KNIGHT needed followers to assist him in peace and in war. At first, pulling a padded coat and mailshirt over the head and lacing a helmet might be all that was required when arming, but putting on plate armour certainly needed assistance. Armour also had to be cared for; mail could be put into a barrel with sand and vinegar and rolled around, allowing the abrasive mixture to spread between the links. Rust needed removing from plate armour – oiling helped to keep air away from the metal when stored. Worn or broken straps or laces had to be replaced.

Squires and pages helped the knight, not only with armour but also in peacetime; 'squires

RIGHT A large curb bit for one of Henry VIII's horses; the horse could play with the rollers and so salivate and froth impressively.

of the body' were closest to their lord. Squires were needed to help look after the horses. A knight used a good, comfortable riding horse, called a palfrey, for training and mounted his destrier when he was about to fight. The destrier (from the word for 'right', meaning either it led with the right leg or was led on the right side) was the most powerful horse, a stallion whose aggression was useful in battle. Some very valuable destriers were used only for the tournament, in which case the knight might use a lesser warhorse, such as the courser. His squires needed mounts, probably easy-going rouncys or hackneys. The knight's equipment was carried on pack horses, called sumpters, or on wagons.

The war horse

Surviving horse armour shows that these horses were generally the size of a modern hunter and early warhorses may have been even smaller. They were specially bred with a deep chest, yet they were nimble in battle. As a result, they were highly expensive; a good warhorse might cost a hundred times the price of a carthorse.

LEFT Late 15th-century South German 'Gothic' armour for a horse; only the rich could afford full horse armour. The rider also wears 'Gothic' armour.

ABOVE A boar badge from a follower of Richard III, found at Bosworth, where the king died in battle against Henry Tudor in 1485.

He might carry armour, clothing, gifts if visiting or attending a tournament, even a portable chapel if moving from one estate to another.

Knights were bound to their lord by feudal duty. At first, they were expected to perform about two months' service in war and 40 days in peace, including castle guard and escort duty. Household knights ate and slept in the lord's castle or manor. For service overseas, contracts were more useful and by the 14th century were replacing feudal service. The retinue expanded into a variable fighting unit called a lance, which might be composed of the knight and squire, several archers who used horses for transport, plus perhaps some foot soldiers. A knight banneret led several lances and a group of bannerets formed a battle, or division. In 1297 Roger Bigod, Earl of Norfolk, led five bannerets, nine knights and 17 men-at-arms.

In the 15th century lords still kept household followers, knights, squires and gentry, now known as 'feed men'. Other retainers (retained or held in the lord's service) lived on their estates, those at some distance being known as 'extraordinary

RIGHT A 12th-century mailed knight mounting his horse ready to go to war.

retainers'. They and their own retained men, such as archers, wore their lord's colours or at least his badge, known as 'Livery and Maintenance'. As in earlier feudal arrangements, men called 'well willers' agreed to serve several lords, so had to make sure they had contracts of employment in case two of their lords went to war. Men sometimes left one lord for another who paid better wages, and this caused pressure on lords and laid emphasis on their wealth. The system, known as 'Bastard Feudalism', contributed to stresses that eventually led the aristocracy into the Wars of the Roses.

11

The basic protection of the earliest knights was the coat of mail, a garment made up of thousands of interlinked iron rings. Each ring was linked through four others and closed with a tiny rivet to strengthen it. Mail was expensive, the coat being shaped by reducing or increasing the number of rings. The coat was often extended into a hood and usually had elbow-length sleeves and a slit up the front and rear, to assist riding. Mail is very flexible but will give under a powerful blow, perhaps resulting in broken bones or severe bruising; therefore it is very likely a padded undergarment, the aketon, was worn underneath. This was made either from two layers of quilted cloth stuffed with cotton, tow, wool or similar, or else from numerous layers of linen. A large wooden shield covered in leather was carried on the left arm, to present a solid defence against weapons. By the mid-11th century, most knightly shields were kite-shaped.

ABOVE Brass of a knight of the Trumpington family, in the church of St Mary and St Michael, Trumpington, Cambridgeshire. His coat-of-arms is repeated on small ailettes at his shoulders. His conical helm is secured to his belt by a long chain.

ABOVE Robert fitzWalter wears a surcoat over mail and a new-style helm with faceguard on his seal, early 13th century. His horse has a long cloth caparison.

A conical iron helmet presented a glancing surface and was usually fitted with a nasal or nose-guard that could stop a sword cut. The prized sword was a broad-bladed, razor-sharp slashing weapon, with a 'fuller' or central channel to lighten the blade without weakening it. A pommel behind the hand helped balance the sword as close to the grip as possible, so the blade was not point heavy. A simple cross guard protected the hand and could act as a crucifix, and the sword was carried in a wood and leather scabbard. A light spear, the lance, was the primary cavalry weapon and used for throwing or stabbing. The idea of tucking or 'couching' it under the arm was in its infancy.

During the 12th century, mail sleeves lengthened and later often extended into mittens, the hand emerging through a slit in the leather palm. Mail leggings or hose became more common. From about 1150 a long cloth surcoat, perhaps copied from Muslim dress, began to be worn over the armour. The shield became flattened at the top and was often convex in shape. Early in the century, couching the lance became usual and the mass charge, knee to knee with levelled lances, was born. A few bronze mace heads, for dealing crushing blows, have survived.

Helmets with faceguards, which had appeared by about 1200, developed in the 13th century into a flat-topped helm covering the whole head. Conical or round-topped helmets, with or without nose-guards, continued but a small skull cap, the cervellière, was often worn over or under the mail hood, itself now sometimes

ABOVE This illustration, c.1200, of the murder of Thomas Becket, shows four knights in mail with large shields, wearing round or cylindrical helmets.

RIGHT A 14th-century mail coat (with later collar) shows the complex construction from thousands of interlinked iron rings. Earlier mail rarely survives.

separate from the mail coat. The kettle hat was an open-brimmed helmet also popular with the infantry, and was useful in hot climates or when climbing scaling ladders. The shield gradually grew smaller in size. By now, some knights wore a solid body defence called the curie, of hardened leather or possibly iron, strapped over their mail but under their surcoat, perhaps a response to arrows with long bodkin points designed to burst mail rings apart. Also, the sword was becoming more tapered and some were sharply pointed. In order to facilitate quick drawing and to minimize tripping, belt fittings became very elaborate. By the late 13th century, the great or 'hand and a half' sword had appeared, a larger weapon usually slung from the saddle. A few knights carried a short axe on horseback, or else a mace, but the lance remained the first weapon in a cavalry charge.

ARMOUR & WEAPONS
1300–1600

The 14th century saw the greatest changes in the development of armour. Already, in the 13th century, plate knee defences, shin defences and elbow defences had appeared. By 1340 most knights wore over their mail the coat-of-plates, or 'plates', a cloth or leather coat inside which were riveted metal plates whose rivet heads were visible on the outer side. By about 1360, the surcoat usually reached the knee and might be quilted; this 'jupon' often bore the owner's heraldic arms. By late century separate breastplates had appeared. The limbs were increasingly protected by gutter-shaped plates on the outer side, then

ABOVE RIGHT The early 15th-century sword from the tomb of Henry V in Westminster Abbey. It is a sharply pointed weapon for both thrusting and cutting.

LEFT Brass of Sir Ralph de Knevyngton at Aveley, Essex, c.1350, showing rivets holding plates under his coat-of-plates and chains to prevent dropping a weapon.

supplemented by hinged tubes and separate plate gauntlets (gloves). A new form of helmet was the basinet, usually pointed and often with a visor and an attached mail collar. Shields were increasingly discarded because plate armour does not yield like mail when struck. Around the same time many knights added a lance-rest to their breastplate, a steel bracket that 'arrests' (stops) the lance from sliding back when striking its target.

Swords were now often quite sharply tapered, for stabbing or slashing, and by the later 14th century the belt was set with gilt or jewelled panels and worn horizontally over the hips. As knights increasingly fought on foot and often discarded the shield, they adopted longer staff weapons, such as large-bladed axes.

By the time of the battle of Agincourt (1415) some knights had done away with the coverings riveted on their plates, and often their jupons. This polished 'alwite' armour was designed to make weapon points slide off. The mail coat was gradually replaced by the arming doublet, a jacket with gussets of mail to defend exposed areas like the armpit, and with lacing points for fastening various pieces of armour. By the mid-15th century complete plate armour, called a 'harness', weighed about 25 kilos (55lbs) (far less than a modern infantryman's back pack). This distributed weight allowed a fit man to run, lie down, mount a horse or even climb the underside of a scaling ladder; however, it becomes very hot. Plate armour was laced and buckled in place, starting at the feet and working up. Once the arming doublet was in place

An expensive suit

Good armour was expensive, and could cost the equivalent of a sports car today. Measurements, even pieces of clothing or wax or wooden models of limbs, were sent to the armourer for a perfect fit. Many knights, however, could not afford this and so obtained their harness (armour) from a merchant armourer. He would have supplies of various components to choose from, and would then alter them as necessary to fit. Some wore a brigandine, rather like a coat-of-plates but with lines of small plates.

a man could be armed from head to foot (cap-a-pie) by two attendants in five minutes.

In the 15th century, several regional styles developed in the great armour-producing centres of Europe. North Italian armour was smooth and rounded, often with a visored armet, which opened at the sides for putting on. Armour made in the German lands became very fluted and elongated in appearance, almost spiky. The usual helmet was the sallet, drawn out to a point at the back, like a sou'wester. Also important were armour centres in Flanders. England had the London Armourers Company, about which little is known. Flemish and English armour was a mixture of the Italian style with some German features, such as the sallet.

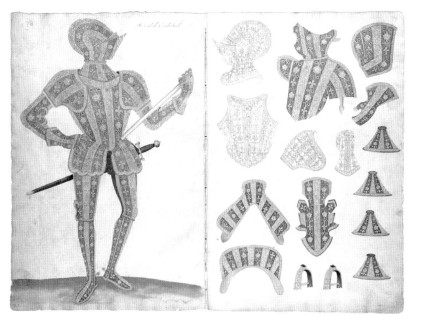

ABOVE The 'Avant' armour, now in the Kelvingrove Art Gallery and Museum, Glasgow, shows the smooth rounded style of Italian armourers in the mid-15th century.

LEFT The design album of Jacob Halder shows the blued, etched and gilt decoration of the finest surviving Greenwich-made armour, c.1580, which belonged to the Earl of Cumberland.

KNIGHTS IN BATTLE

CAVALRY at first dominated warfare but disciplined foot soldiers and well placed archers could break a mounted charge. Warfare often consisted of burning an enemy's crops and villages, damaging his economy and demonstrating that he could not protect his people. In the Hundred Years War in France, the large-scale raid or 'chevauchée' was this type of warfare. Set piece battles were risky affairs and were not especially common.

Norman knights followed the pennon (a small flag) on their lord's lance, riding up to throw or stab with their light lances, while a few tucked them under the arm. However, at Hastings in 1066 they came up against the shield wall of the Anglo-Danes and the great two-handed axe used in the north. It took all day to break the English line using a combination of archers, foot soldiers and cavalry and some, perhaps unintentional, withdrawals that lured Englishmen from their hilltop. Increasingly on the battlefield, dismounted knights stiffened ranks of infantry, as at the later Battle of the Standard against the Scots, in 1139.

ABOVE The Battle of Agincourt (1415) from a later 15th-century illustration. Stabbing swords are evident and arrows from longbows inflict deep wounds on the horses.

ABOVE The Bayeux Tapestry shows mailed English thegns and housecarls confronting mounted Norman knights with great axes, at Hastings in 1066.

Edward I (1272–1307) was a great military leader. He built massive castles in Wales, then he invaded Scotland. At Stirling Bridge, in 1297, William Wallace fell upon the English when about a third of the army had crossed the river, leaving the rest harmlessly on the other bank. Next year, at Falkirk, the Scots formed schiltrons, hedgehogs of long spears to hold off cavalry but King Edward personally took charge, and brought up his archers and crossbowmen to pour a stream of missiles into the schiltrons, which could not break formation for fear of a cavalry charge. Once weakened, the knights charged in. Edward II found the same problem at the battle of Bannockburn, in 1314, but Scottish horsemen caught his archers unprepared and knights attacking the schiltrons were pushed into marshy ground.

The Hundred Years War with France commenced in 1337. Edward III had used longbowmen standing with dismounted knights four years earlier, at Halidon Hill in Scotland,

RIGHT A 15th-century illustration shows the chaos of mounted warfare. After the initial clash, the lance was dropped in favour of swords, maces or axes.

the Scottish charge being broken up by arrows. Cavalry were used to lead a decisive charge, or for chasing the enemy as they fled, when much of the killing would take place. Edward now took these tactics to France. The English ideally protected themselves with hedges and ditches in a position where they could not be outflanked.

The first major battle using these tactics was Crécy in 1346, where Edward's small army was heavily outnumbered; French knights were mown down by arrows and those reaching the English line were beaten off until they finally withdrew. The Black Prince, the eldest son of Edward III, launched a chevauchée, or mounted raid, that was cornered at Poitiers in 1356. Hard pressed by dismounted knights, the prince mounted a reserve and led in a flank attack, capturing the French sovereign, King John, in the process. Later, the French simply avoided battle with the English, unless they could catch the archers out of position, as at Patay in 1429.

When the Wars of the Roses broke out in 1455, knights still largely fought on foot. Unlike much medieval warfare, when ransom was a lucrative way to gain riches by taking noblemen as prisoners, the Wars of the Roses presented opportunities to settle old scores. By the 16th century, knights often acted as captains or officers. It is worth noting that battles always remained a last resort, because they were unpredictable. Sieges were considered the best way to wage war.

LEFT The charge of mounted knights riding close together with levelled lances was a fearsome weapon.

Henry V's great victory

At Agincourt in 1415, Henry V used archers and dismounted knights to defeat a force at least twice that of his own. His archers carried sharpened stakes to place in front of them as a defence against cavalry, and Agincourt Wood and Tramecourt Wood, on either side of the battlefield and flanking the positions, prevented outflanking. The main battle was fought by dismounted knights on both sides.

The origins of the science of heraldry are obscure, since men have always used symbols to identify themselves. Norman shields on the Bayeux Tapestry are painted with designs, such as lions and crosses. However, heraldry differs, in that the symbol adopted by a person is unique to him, and is inherited by his eldest son. This first use of images for knights seems to occur from about 1135. This is around the same time that

RIGHT An illustration of the helm and lion crest of Edward, the Black Prince. The originals are preserved in Canterbury Cathedral.

the first tournaments were being established, and it is quite possible that heraldry grew up to assist identification of knights in these contests, rather than during battle.

It used to be thought that heraldry arose because knights could not be recognized as the helmet increasingly covered the face, but at Hastings in 1066 Duke William had to throw his helmet back to identify himself to his men, when they thought he was dead; in any case knights were using symbols for recognition long before the birth of heraldry.

At first, the main use of heraldry was on the shield. Symbols placed there are called 'arms' and are the personal mark of the owner. Popular early figures were lions and eagles, while geometric designs were also common, but many subjects were used, from stars to corn stooks. In order to make the design stand out, white and yellow (representing the 'metals': silver and gold) could not be placed on top of one another; nor could a colour (mainly red, blue or black to begin with) be placed on another colour.

Soon arms were being used on other items. The long, plain surcoat was an ideal place but, surprisingly, this was not especially popular until the 14th century. It gave the term 'coat-of-arms', which now refers to the arms themselves. They were also carried on a knight's pennon, the small triangular flag sometimes carried at the tip of his lance. A knight promoted to banneret (and thus

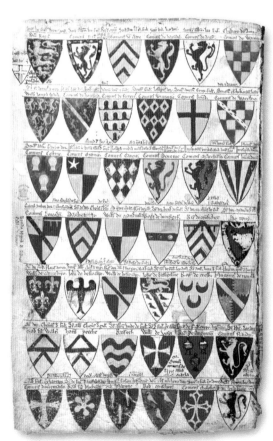

ABOVE Heraldic coats-of-arms, from the *Liber Additamentorum* of Matthew Paris, *c.*1244. Rolls of arms were also compiled by heralds for themselves and for a patron, plus occasional rolls for special occasions such as a tournament.

LEFT Standard of Edward IV, bearing elements of his arms and heraldic colours. The king's standards were carried as rallying flags for his troops.

in charge of other knights) had a banner, a square or rectangular flag that marked him out in the field; when a knight did well in battle, his pennon might have its tail cut off to form a makeshift banner. The long standard that appeared around the 14th century carried elements of a lord's arms, and many also had a cross of St George; this marked the rallying point for his men. The horse's cloth caparison, or trapper, appearing in the late 12th century, was also used for heraldic display.

ABOVE Sir Geoffrey Luttrell and family, from the Luttrell Psalter, c.1340. Arms were worn on surcoats, horses' caparisons, lance pennons, dress, books, plate, even liturgical vestments.

Lords at first chose their own arms and tried to avoid clashing with other families, although within related families arms might simply vary to show the connection – for example, in the colour, or in the number of chevrons. In England, eldest sons began to 'difference' their father's arms with a mark, often a 'label' – a narrow horizontal band with pendant tabs – which was removed when a son inherited. Younger sons also differenced their arms.

ABOVE Richard II in this late 15th-century illustration wears a heraldic tabard, the royal arms repeated on his personal banner.

Heralds & history

Heralds, first mentioned in French texts in the 12th century, were initially 'marshals and messengers of the tournament, masters of ceremonies and makers of minstrelsy'. Later, they also had functions in war as messengers and in identifying and recording casualties. Heralds worked for lords, as well as for the king, and by the end of the 14th century they were compiling rolls of arms (earlier painted rolls were part of chronicled histories). In the 15th century, the royal heralds gained control over the granting of arms.

✚ ORDERS OF KNIGHTHOOD ✚

At first, knights formed a brotherhood because of their status. The oldest class, known as 'the bachelery of England' was made up of 'knights bachelor', usually landless knights not part of an Order of chivalry, or young knights following the banners of others. The early Orders of chivalry were not secular but religious. In or near 1119, Hugh of Payns gathered some knights in the Holy Land (Jerusalem) to protect pilgrims on journeys to the Holy Places. As warrior monks, the Order of the Temple became known as the Templars after the Temple Mount, where they had their headquarters. Trained and armed as mounted knights, they became some of the

ABOVE The circular chancel of Temple Church, London, English headquarters of the Order of the Temple.

LEFT The foundation of the French Order of the Star, by John the Good, from the *Chroniques de France*, late 14th century.

most disciplined warriors of their day. In about 1126, the Knights of St John, who had been providing medical care for years, were formed. These Orders had preceptories (houses) in England and elsewhere, recruited knights and received donations; English recruits tended to join the Knights Hospitaller.

Secular Orders of chivalry first appear in a proposal by Edward III in 1344, at Windsor Castle, for an Order of the Round Table. Then King John of France submitted a proposal for an Order of the Star, but this was delayed by war with England (it finally emerged in 1351–52 but was more or less destroyed by the French military disaster at Poitiers.) Thus in 1348, the Order of the Garter became Europe's first knightly Order, and remains its oldest. Edward III is said to have been dancing with Joan, Countess of Salisbury when her blue silk garter fell down; in order to save her embarrassment the king picked it up and placed it on his own leg, with the words 'Honi soit qui mal y pense' ('Shame on him who thinks this shameful'). It is quite possible the motto refers to Edward's pretensions to the French crown and is aimed at his critics, whilst the colours echo the French royal flag; there is much evidence of ideas taken from the scheme for the Order of the Star.

The Order of the Garter had the king at its head and a set number of 25 knights, new knights being recruited only when a seat became available. Many of the first members were companions of the king in his French wars. Its badge was a blue silk garter with the motto in gold letters along it,

which knights wore on their left leg, even over their armour. Garments were also designed for members, including a surcoat, mantle and hood, with a cap and collar introduced in the reign of Henry VII. By the early 15th century, a blue mantle with a cross of St George within a garter was being worn. Henry V created the heraldic office of Garter King of Arms, today the senior English King of Arms.

The Order of the Bath reflects the ritual bath undertaken by aspirants before being knighted. By the 14th century, this had become a ritual when part of an event such as a coronation, participants being known as Knights of the Bath from at least the early 15th century although not organized as an Order. Having fallen into disuse in about 1660, the Order of the Bath appeared in 1725. In Burgundy, France, the Order of the Golden Fleece, founded in 1430 and marked by the badge of a hanging fleece, became the greatest Order in Europe. Some smaller European Orders were set up in the 14th and 15th centuries by knights as a whim, perhaps for charitable purposes.

✦ JOUSTS & TOURNAMENTS ✦

The tournament began as a training for war, probably in the 12th century, and refers to the wheeling manoeuvres performed by knights competing in a mock battle. It was usually a battle over a wide area of countryside between two teams of mounted knights, sometimes assisted by foot soldiers. The idea was to capture opponents, who must forfeit horse and armour or pay a ransom, so skilled fighters could make their fortune, as indeed did the landless younger son, William Marshal (see page 26). His biography mentions knights ganging up on one another or even pretending not to take part, and then rushing in at the crucial moment. Real weapons were used and, not surprisingly, there were many casualties. Popular in France, tournaments were at first banned in England, partly because kings feared their use as a cover for revolt.

During the 13th century, tournaments were increasingly held in a large arena (the 'lists') and provided with stands for the spectators; blunted weapons became more common and a new form of combat, the joust between two mounted knights, gained popularity, partly because a knight could demonstrate his prowess without distraction. The sharp lance for jousting 'a outrance' proved courage and skill but many preferred jousting 'a plaisance', using a blunt head or a coronel of small points to spread the blow. At first, unhorsing an opponent was the aim but, especially with blunted lances, breaking the lance well against the opponent became important. Dangers, especially

LEFT A joust of war with sharp lances before Richard II, from a manuscript dating from the late 15th century.

RIGHT Queen Catherine of Aragon watches Henry VIII in jousts of peace at Westminster, in 1511.

from flying wooden splinters, encouraged the development of specialized armour, notably the 'frog-mouthed' helm in the 14th century, where the lower edge of the vision slit jutted forward in line with the upper edge, to protect the eyes.

Until the early 15th century all jousts were run 'in the open' with no barrier, but a powerful horse could ride down an opponent, or riders' knees would collide on a close pass. Often horses ran wide and knights missed completely. Then, a barrier became common. This 'tilt', which gave its name to such contests, guided the riders and meant the lances struck at a greater angle, with more chance of breaking. Jousts with sharp lances were still often run without a barrier. Styles developed in different countries, with German lands slow to adopt the tilt.

Occasionally jousters could dismount, to continue on foot. During the 14th century foot combats with special armour became a feature in their own right and by the 16th century foot tourneys – two teams fighting across a barrier with pikes and blunt swords – became popular. For these combats 'hitting below the belt' was forbidden, so leg armour was often omitted.

The mounted team event, the tourney, remained a popular spectacle and one form, the baston course, only permitted clubs or blunt swords. An event seen especially in the 15th century was the 'pas d'armes', where a position (a designated piece of ground) was held against all comers; themes from legends were woven into a theatrical spectacle, with artificial golden trees, shepherdesses, giants and dwarves.

ABOVE Robert Radcliffe, Earl of Sussex (1593), dressed for foot combat. Notice the lack of leg armour and the elaborate feathered helmet.

The tournament declined in the 17th century, the pike-wielding foot tourneys a reminder of the pikes now coming to the fore on the battlefield. As the armoured knight passed into history, so the tournament was largely replaced by the carrousel – displays of horsemanship, or riding at a suspended ring with a lance.

Ladies' day

Elaborate rules developed around the tournament. Heralds delivered challenges and recorded contestants, who often accepted by touching shields which were coloured to represent different combats. Scores could be kept on 'jousting cheques'. Ladies increasingly became a central part of the whole event; a lady of the tournament might present the prize but could also have a dishonourable knight removed. Knights wore ladies' favours, such as tokens from their dresses, or a sleeve or veil, and, by the time of Elizabeth I, contestants spouted poetry for her delight.

✦ The Code of Chivalry ✦

To the early knight 'chivalry' meant his prowess in horsemanship, rather than devotion to a lady. The Bayeux Tapestry has very few women represented compared to horses, a trend also found in contemporary epic poems, the *chansons de geste*. The spread of the ideals of courtly love in the 12th century, and the contemporary cult of the Virgin Mary, which put the lady to the fore, led to a softening attitude towards women, whether or not it reflected real life: in the feudal world, knights were keen to marry rich heiresses in order to obtain land.

Lives of real heroes were celebrated in songs by minstrels and also formed the basis for books written to explain the code of chivalry. The most famous edition, Ramon Llull's *Le libre del Ordre de Cavelleria* (*c.*1265), was translated into English and printed, in 1484, by William Caxton as *The Ordre of Chyvalry or Knyghthode*. Some of these works were a reminder to knights of what chivalry meant. Based on Llull, Alain Chartier made a list of virtues: nobility, loyalty, honour, righteousness, prowess, love, courtesy, diligence, cleanliness, generosity, sobriety and perseverance.

The Church had always tried to civilize early knights by invoking such ideals as the Truce of God, to prohibit violence on certain days, but it was hard work. However, perseverance had its reward, and Church attitudes increasingly influenced the ceremony of knighting, to include a vigil at the altar, blessing of the sword and a ritual bath to wash away sins. Castle chaplains might teach squires to read and write. The 12th-century St Bernard berated knights and their rich apparel, contrasting them with the Templar warrior monks. Churchmen riled at the violence of the tournament and prophesied dire punishments in the next life. They saw the Crusades not only as a chance to win back the Holy Land but also a way of channelling knightly aggression away from Europe.

NOBILITY
LOYALTY
HONOUR
RIGHTEOUSNESS
PROWESS
LOVE
COURTESY
DILIGENCE
CLEANLINESS
GENEROSITY
SOBRIETY
PERSEVERANCE

LEFT Fully armoured, Lord Edward Despenser kneels in prayer, from a 14th-century carving in Tewkesbury Abbey, Gloucestershire whose chantry chapel of Holy Trinity he built.

ABOVE Lovers in conversation, from an exquisite carved ivory mirror case of about 1320, in the Louvre, Paris.

King Arthur & his knights

Stories of King Arthur grew in popularity and the 'finding' of Arthur's tomb at Glastonbury in 1191 was supported by King Richard I, a French Angevin monarch identifying himself with a British predecessor. Arthur and his knights became very popular figures in English legend and 'Round Table' entertainments were held in the 13th and 14th centuries, notably in a great festival in 1344 at Windsor Castle.

Jean Froissart does not question Edward's right to do so. A good ransom was also a huge incentive to keep a knight alive, of course. Similarly, mercenary knights and 'Free Companies' fought for pay and were not too concerned about codes of behaviour. Yet, there were decent men who fought with honour and upheld all that was good about knighthood and chivalry.

Knighthood itself was like a club: only those of a certain standing could enter it, and across Europe knights grew to recognize renowned names, sometimes by visiting tournaments, especially during the 14th and 15th centuries. Good fighters earned respect, and captured knights might be given parole on their word not to escape. This atmosphere contributed to Chaucer's 'verray parfit gentil knight', a man gracious to his enemies, courteous to ladies, protector of the Church and the weak.

However, this ideal did not always apply when tempers frayed, especially during a long siege, nor did it sometimes extend to ordinary folk. In 1370 the Bishop of Limoges, a friend of Edward, the Black Prince, deserted the English army and joined the French. The irate Edward sacked the town, killing men, women and children. In describing the incident, the chronicler

Through great deeds some knights gained recognition in their day and have remained famous for hundreds of years.

William Marshal was born about 1144, a landless younger son trained in the household of a powerful cousin, William of Tancarville, and knighted by him when 20 years old, on the eve of battle. He fought well during a skirmish at Drincourt in France but took no spoils of war, prompting comments that he fought like an ideal knight but could little afford not to be a real

ABOVE This effigy, c.1230, in Temple Church, London, is often said to be that of William Marshal, who died in 1219.

ABOVE The seal of King Richard I (Lionheart) (ruled 1189–99), a great fighter, good military leader and Crusader but not especially interested in governing England.

knight because he needed money to live. He made a fortune from ransoms by capturing knights in tournaments, and tutored Henry II's eldest son. Eventually, William became Earl of Pembroke, serving Richard I and King John and becoming Regent for the infant Henry III.

Sir William Longespée (Longsword), eldest son of the Earl of Salisbury, was knighted when

RIGHT The effigy of Edward, the Black Prince (died 1376), in Canterbury Cathedral. His name may refer to the black coat-of-arms for jousts of peace, on his tomb.

about 21 and twice joined the Crusades. In 1249, at Mansourah in Egypt, the headstrong Robert of Artois demanded an immediate attack but the Grand Master of the Templars and Sir William advised that they wait for King Louis to join them. Insulted by Robert as cowards, Sir William snapped: 'Count Robert! I will go so far in danger today that you shall not even dare to touch the tail of my horse.' Charging into the town, the Egyptians closed the gates to cut off the Crusaders. Sir William was mortally wounded in the ensuing battle but fought on, refusing to surrender, until he was finally killed.

Sir James Douglas received the heart of his friend, Robert the Bruce after his death in 1329,

ABOVE A funerary monument of 1436 to English mercenary captain Sir John Hawkwood, in the Duomo, Florence, by Uccello.

to be taken to the Holy Land. Sir James, known as 'The Good', set out on his journey but as he travelled through Spain he decided to help the King of Castile, who was fighting the Moors. Sir James was wounded and knew he could not hope to fulfil his mission, so he flung the casket containing the heart into the ranks of the Muslims, with the cry: 'Go first as thou were wont to go.' The Douglas family was later awarded a heart device to add to their coat-of-arms.

Sir John Chandos was one of the most famous knights, awarded the Order of the Garter by Edward III, for chivalry and courage. He fought at Crécy with the Black Prince and, at Poitiers, urged him to seek out the French king. Fighting at Mortemer in France, in 1370, he caught his legs in the long robe over his armour and skidded on the frosty ground. His visor was up and a French squire, James de St Martin, made a lance thrust at his face. Failing to see it because one eye was blinded from a hunting accident, he fell on the point and died soon afterwards. He was mourned by both armies. The chronicler Froissart wrote: 'For never since a hundred years did there exist among the English one more courteous, nor fuller of every virtue and good quality than him.'

Sir John Hawkwood began life as a tailor and earned the nickname 'Needle John'. Soldiering was more to his taste and he took part in the Hundred Years War, leading a group called the 'White Company' or 'White Brotherhood' because of their clothing. During a lull in hostilities, he led his men down to Italy, where he fought as a mercenary, joining whichever side was likely to win. When two friars wished him peace, he cursed them: 'Do you not know that I live by war and peace would be my undoing?' He died in 1394.

✦ KNIGHTS IN LITERATURE ✦

The first knights heard of heroic deeds in the *chansons de geste*, epic tales full of stirring battles. The most famous, *The Song of Roland*, was supposedly sung by Taillefer, one of the Norman knights who fought at the battle of Hastings in 1066. It was not until the 12th century, in the courts of southern France, that songs of love began to be spread by troubadours, promoted by the powerful Eleanor of Aquitaine. The queen taught poetry to her son, Richard, soon to be known as 'Lionheart'. The troubadours sang of unrequited love, of a knight yearning for an often unattainable lady – courtly love. The popularity of the troubadours' songs moved north, where the trouvères sang slightly more robust songs, and spread to the German poets, the Minnesingers.

The most famous warriors were King Arthur and his knights of the Round Table. Celtic stories of Arthur, a shadowy figure from the 5th or 6th century, were written down in 1135 by

ABOVE The Holy Grail appears before the Knights of the Round Table, from a 15th-century illustration.

Geoffrey of Monmouth as part of the *History of the Kings of Britain* but much of the romance and characterization was added in the writings of Chrétien de Troyes in the late 12th century. By 1240, many of the stories had been compiled together as prose, presenting Arthur and his followers in the knightly world familiar to the writers of the Arthurian stories. Woven into these romances are tales of dragons and magic, including that of the Green Knight who survives being beheaded by Sir Gawain, the most popular Arthurian hero in England. The stories were collected by Sir Thomas Malory in 1450–60, who translated them into English because many knights could no longer read French.

The Arthurian romances gradually became morally more high minded. *The Quest of the Holy Grail* was probably written to bring chivalry under the authority of the Church; said to have been brought to England, only Galahad, the purest knight, finally achieves the Grail. The heroes of King Arthur's court were the dispensers of

ABOVE The Round Table on the wall in the Great Hall, Winchester Castle. The table actually dates to the 13th century but was overpainted in the early 16th century.

ABOVE Sir Perceval, Sir Bors and Sir Galahad (kneeling) see the Grail, from *The Quest for the Holy Grail*, by Sir Edward Burne-Jones (1894). The Pre-Raphaelite artists were attracted to the Arthurian legends.

RIGHT A tournament, illustrated in a 15th-century re-telling of the stories of King Arthur and the Knights of the Round Table, written by Chrétien de Troyes.

justice and representatives of chivalry. Among the greatest, Tristan searched out adventures as a knight-errant and loved Iseult, for the lady remained at the centre of the knightly world.

Other writers preferred to recall the deeds of real people. William Marshal's colourful career (see page 26) was written down at the end of the old man's life, by a jongleur, helped by William's squire, and provides a detailed glimpse of a successful knight's career in the 12th century. Jean Froissart, in his famous *Chronicles*, described at length the deeds of knights living in the second half of the 14th century, mainly those from France and England.

One such warrior was Sir Walter Manny, the son of a Frenchman, who came to England as squire to Philippa of Hainault, the bride of Edward III. Walter was knighted three years later and fought well in the Scottish wars, and in the sea battle against the French, off Sluys, in 1340. During a siege at Guingamp, he went out after dinner and destroyed a siege engine before unhorsing French knights. King Edward fought incognito under Sir Walter's banner in 1348. In 1371 he founded the Charterhouse, a Carthusian monastery, in London.

Chandos Herald (an English herald) wrote a biography of the Black Prince and others were written of gallant French knights, including

Bertrand du Guesclin and, in more romantic mode, Marshal Boucicault, Jacques de Lalain and Chevalier Bayart. Reality and romance were often blurred, and even much earlier Classical stories were given a knightly treatment. There were also handbooks on chivalric behaviour, written to revive chivalry and brave deeds. But times were changing. Elizabethan Englishmen now read *The Book of the Courtier* by the Italian writer Castiglione, where the new gentleman was no longer interested in chivalry. The reputation of medieval knights would be rescued by the Victorian writers and artists in the 19th century.

In the 16th century chivalry was at its most flamboyant in the pomp of Henry VIII's meeting with Francis I of France, at the Field of Cloth of Gold in 1520, and seen in deeds such as the Earl of Essex thrusting a pike into the gates of Lisbon, to offer single combat on behalf of his mistress, in 1589. However, in Protestant England medieval chivalry was associated with Catholicism and was becoming a relic in the age of the Renaissance, where realism and order were encouraged. Chivalry was lost in Puritan England until the romantic view of knighthood reappeared in the 19th century.

In the Wars of the Roses (1455–85) confrontations took the form of battles, with relatively few sieges, and by the 16th century England was largely at peace; garrisoned forts took the place of the castle for defence, and now men chose to build country houses with little or no protection, purely as residences.

By the time of the English Civil Wars, the armoured cavalryman was outmoded on the battlefield. Soldiers were mostly troopers; their armour was becoming heavy, since ideally helmet

and breastplate needed to be proofed against bullets as gunpowder became more effective. Armoured lancers carried a lance but their usefulness on the battlefield was limited, since large infantry

ABOVE Henry V and his victory at Agincourt was immortalized by Shakespeare. The 1944 film version, with Laurence Olivier, roused England during the Second World War.

BELOW The extravagant meeting near Calais in 1520 of Henry VIII of England and Francis I of France became known as the Field of Cloth of Gold.

formations carried hedges of 16-foot (4.9-m) pikes, through which they were unable to penetrate, and they were shot down by musketeers. Armoured cuirassiers carrying pistols disappeared in 1643, routed by royalist harquebusiers at the Battle of Roundway Down, near Devizes in Wiltshire. The lighter harquebusiers wore only breast and back plates, or a coat of buff leather; they galloped up with wheellock pistols, fired and rode away.

Knighthood was now largely a mark of rank. Knights might fight as officers but equally could concentrate on peaceful duties; the lord of the manor was now the country squire. Attitudes to courtly love were changing. Already by the 15th century, the love of a lady was seen as a distraction to chivalry. From obscure medieval beginnings the Scottish Order of the Thistle was revived in 1687 and the Order of the Bath in 1725. New orders of chivalry, such as the Order of St Michael and St George and the Royal Victorian Order, came into being.

The Victorian Pre-Raphaelites and their successors illustrated medieval stories. A great tournament was reconstructed at Eglinton, in Scotland, in 1839 but was effectively washed away by a thunderstorm. In the 20th century, knightly ideals were used to inspire victory in the First World War and similarly, in the Second World War, with the famous film version of Shakespeare's *Henry V* and his victory against the odds at the battle of Agincourt.

As television came of age in the 1950s, children's series included *Sir Lancelot*, *The Black Knight* and *Ivanhoe*; Sir Walter Scott's *Ivanhoe* has been made into a film and several TV versions. Robin Hood has seen innumerable revivals, while King Arthur remains a perennial favourite. Jousting was revived in the 1960s, and now re-enactors in ever more faithful armour regularly replicate tournaments and medieval battles for the public's enjoyment. Nowadays, the Knights of the Garter continue to process to St George's Chapel at Windsor Castle in full regalia. Knighthood today is bestowed by the sovereign for service, and is still symbolized by tapping the kneeling recipient on the shoulder with a sword. It remains the highest honour that can be given, below those of the peerage. A knight's wife receives the title of 'Lady' but if a female receives the honour on her own merits, the equivalent reward is to become a dame. The knightly world will never fade, and the instinct for fair play and honourable behaviour is still expected of the true gentleman.

RIGHT The grand tournament hosted by Lord Eglinton in 1839 turned into a washout thanks to the British weather.

PLACES TO VISIT

THERE are many castles, cathedrals, abbeys and manor houses in Britain, as well as museums displaying medieval objects, and battlefield sites. English Heritage and the National Trust look after a huge number and all of these can be visited. In Wales, Cadw care for some of the greatest castles ever built in Britain.

Alnwick Castle, Alnwick, Northumberland NE66 1NQ
01665 510777;
www.alnwickcastle.com

Arundel Castle, Arundel, West Sussex BN18 9AB
01903 882173; www.arundelcastle.org/_pages/01_castle.htm

British Museum, Great Russell Street, London WC1B 3DG
020 7323 8000/8299;
www.britishmuseum.org

Canterbury Cathedral, The Precincts, Canterbury, Kent CT1 2EH
01227 762862;
www.canterbury-cathedral.org/

Cardiff Castle, Castle Street, Cardiff, South Glamorgan CF10 3RB
029 2087 8100;
www.cardiffcastle.com

Hedingham Castle, Castle Hedingham, Essex CO9 3DJ
01787 460261;
www.hedinghamcastle.co.uk

Ludlow Castle, Castle Square, Ludlow, Shropshire SY8 1AY
01584 873355;
www.ludlowcastle.com

Pembroke Castle, Pembroke, Pembrokeshire SA71 4LA
01646 684585;
www.pembroke-castle.co.uk

Royal Armouries Museum, Armouries Drive, Leeds, West Yorkshire LS10 1LT
0113 220 1999;
www.royalarmouries.org/

Temple Church, Temple Place, City of London EC4Y 7HL
020 7353 3470;
www.templechurch.com/

Tower of London, Tower Hill, London EC3N 4AB
020 7488 5663;
www.hrp.org.uk/toweroflondon

Warwick Castle, Warwick, Warwickshire CV34 4QU
0871 265 2000;
www.warwick-castle.co.uk

Westminster Abbey, Parliament Square, London SW1P 3PA
020 7222 5152;
www.westminster-abbey.org

The Great Hall, The Castle, Winchester, Hampshire SO23 8PJ
01962 846476;
www3.hants.gov.uk/greathall

Windsor Castle, Windsor, Berkshire SL4 1NJ
020 7766 7304; www.royalcollection.org.uk and follow the link

Llywodraeth Cynulliad Cymru
Welsh Assembly Government

www.cadw.wales.gov.uk and follow the Places to Visit link

Beaumaris Castle, Anglesey LL58 8AP
0248 810361; www.beaumaris.com

Caernarfon Castle, Caernarfon, Gwynedd LL55 2AY
01286 677617

Caerphilly Castle, Caerphilly, Glamorgan CF83 1JD
029 2088 3143

ABOVE Tower of London.

Chepstow Castle, Chepstow, Monmouthshire NP16 5EY
01291 624065

Conwy Castle, 5 Rose Hill Street, Conwy LL32 8AY
01492 592358

Harlech Castle, near Barmouth, Gwynedd LL46 2YH
01766 780552

ENGLISH HERITAGE

Battle Abbey, High Street, Battle, East Sussex TN33 0AD
01424 775705/0870 333 1181;
www.englishheritage.org.uk/battleabbey

Dover Castle, Castle Hill, Dover, Kent CT16 1HU
01304 211067; www.english-heritage.org.uk/dovercastle

Warkworth Castle, Castle Terrace, Warkworth, Northumberland NE65 0UJ
01665 711 423; www.english-heritage.org.uk/warkworth-castle-and-hermitage/

National Trust

Bodiam Castle, Bodiam, East Sussex TN32 5UA
01580 830196;
www.nationaltrust.org.uk

Information correct at time of going to press.

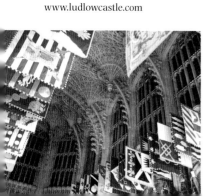

LEFT Henry VII Chapel, Westminster Abbey.